POSTCARDS
IN A CLOSET

A Creative Non-Fiction Memoir

Lori Wolf-Heffner

Postcards in a Closet: A Creative Non-Fiction
Memoir

Book Design by Angela Donelle –
angeladonelle.com

E-book ISBN-13: 978-0-9950906-1-3

Print book ISBN-13: 978-0-9950906-0-6

Published by Head in the Ground Publishing
Waterloo, Ontario, Canada

Dedicated to the Danube Swabians from Eastern Europe, whose stories are now spread throughout the world.

Acknowledgements

For most of 2015, I participated in a mentorship program organized by the Canadian Senior Artists' Resource Network (CSARN). My mentor, writer Carol McCuaig, offered her advice and feedback throughout the year and was instrumental in helping me complete this project. Thank you, Carol.

I also owe a thank you to my husband, Corey, and my two sons, Khristopher and Jonnathan, who all frequently heard the phrase "I have to write" as I disappeared into our office, sometimes with a handful of chocolate, and closed both doors to work on this project (and many others).

Thank yous go out to my mom and aunt for giving me permission to publish this book.

And lastly, I'd like to thank Katharina Wolf, my great grandmother, who proved just how powerful writing can be. If she hadn't written those postcards, her life would've disappeared into the sands of time.

Introduction

Katharina Wolf was born on April 8, 1901, in a Hungarian hamlet called Scheiting, but lived her life—so far as I can tell—in neighbouring Semlak. I don't know when Katharina died. At some point in time, she moved to a nearby city. It could have been Arad, which is only 37 km away. However, I suspect she chose Temeswar (whose inner core used to be called "Little Vienna"), though it's almost 100 km away from Semlak. Mom also told me that Katharina loved modern things, and Temeswar would fit the bill for someone who loved the conveniences and fashions of modern life. Some pictures of Katharina in her later years are also in Temeswar. Based on what Mom and I could piece together, Katharina died in a summer between 1961 and 1965 in whichever city she was living in. Katharina wrote about problems with her blood pressure, and heart and stroke problems can be found in both her ancestors and descendants. Those clues plus a few more details from Mom's recollections led me to believe that Katharina most likely died from a heart attack or stroke.

Katharina's first 44 years were marred by the storm of events in the first half of the 20th century: both World Wars, dictatorship, and the rise of Communism. Living in Eastern Europe, she would twice experience being caught on the war front between Germany and Russia. After World War II, Romania became Communist and Katharina lived the remainder of her life under a dictatorship, separated from her family by the Iron Curtain. Her mail was even inspected by government authorities, as was routine in those regimes. Trapped in her own country, she couldn't leave to travel, nor could her family travel to her. In several postcards, she wrote how she cried because she couldn't see her grandchildren.

The following is a small collection of fictitious journal entries heavily based on Katharina's own postcards, my research, and my own experiences as an expectant mother. I think, in the end, we're not as different as we'd like to believe we are.

Letters to
My Child

Monday, July 18, 1921

My dear child,

 As I await your arrival, I'm going to write down stories about life in Semlak, the village your family has lived in for 100 years now.

 Until 1919, Semlak belonged to Hungary, which was part of the Austro-Hungarian Empire. Now, we belong to Romania, and I don't know how much things will change. I don't know what language they'll teach you in school. When I went to school, we learned Hungarian and very little German. Will you have to learn Romanian, then? How will I help you with your schoolwork? And what kind of job will you have? How will the Romanians treat us Germans? And what about our faith? Hungarians are Lutheran; Romanians are Catholic or even Orthodox. Will we Germans have to move again because of our faith?

 So I want you to learn about your family and your culture. Times are changing in Europe. I know life will never be the same as it was before the War.

Your Mammi

Friday, August 12, 1921

My dear child,

It's raining today. I hope it rains well — the plants need more water. A good harvest gives us health and life.

Whether you're a girl or boy, you'll learn how to farm. You'll have two plots of land to look after: the farmland outside our village and the garden behind our house.

At the front of the house, we have an acacia tree. They grow fast and can be cut down if wood is needed. In our gardens in the back, we have pear and peach trees. Mama makes a wonderful peach cake in the summer when the peaches are ripe. The rest we preserve and store in the fruit cellar.

Gardening and farming are hard work, but it's the German way. You'll also learn how to grow grapes for wine. Most years, you'll have enough food to eat and wine to celebrate, and you can sell any extra at the market in Arad. We're lucky that Tata is a blacksmith — it's helped our family earn more money. But most trades are for Hungarians, and I suppose Romanians, at least the few that live in our village. As a German, you will likely earn your keep through farming.

I think you'll love working outside all the time. I don't know what child doesn't. But will you love to get dirty? Or will you want to stay clean? I think children are simply born with a love or hate for dirt.

Either way, I'll teach you how to be clean, because that's so very important. You must always have clean, polished shoes. Your clothing must be pressed. Sometimes I hope you're a boy so you won't have to worry about pressing your clothes – it's so tedious! A good wife will do that for you. Plus, I won't have to press your many underskirts when you're old enough to wear them.

It's time for me to go outside and bring in the laundry. I'll be spending the better part of the afternoon ironing Mama's underskirts so they're freshly starched for church on Sunday.

Your Mammi

Friday, September 2, 1921

My dear child,

    Let me tell you about my Tata, your Wolf Ota. He was a hard worker, like all Lutheran Semlakers, and became a blacksmith. His ancestors were farmers, just like most of the people in the village.

    Tata tried travelling twice to Amerika to find work. He had heard that he might be able to earn between 500 and 1,200 dollars a year, which is about 3,000 to 60,000 crowns. (With our land, I think we only earned about 1,000 crowns a year.) Then he'd bring some of that home and buy more farmland for the family to work. He first went when I was a young girl. I think I was six. Mama worked on our small farm and also helped out at larger farms to make sure we had enough to eat. She earned 20 crowns a year for her work, plus 20 hundredweights of grain, and salt, vinegar, bacon, and firewood. Even though my brother Adam and I were still children, we had to help with the farm work, and I had to help look after my three sisters, who were very young. (Your Onkel Adam is two years older than me.)

I was really scared that something would happen to Tata. Amerika is so far away. He had to first travel to Arad, take a train to Temeswar and then Budapest, and then take another one all the way to Hamburg in the German Empire. He travelled over 1,200 km, and he hadn't even got on a ship yet. He said they speak a different German there, but he could get by. I know Mama was very scared, too. There were five of us at home and no father. We didn't see him much because of his work, but we at least knew he was there.

When Tata went to Amerika again, I was 12. I remember clearly: As he was washing up, his mother, my Wolf Omama, knelt before him and with all her strength held Tata at his feet, and she kissed both and stroked her son as she cried. "I won't see you again my child," she said. And that's how it was.

This was only one year after the great ship Titanic sank, so I was very frightened something would happen to him. I had to wait for several weeks before he got word to us that he'd arrived safely.

If you go to Amerika, I have one request: that you take me with you. As much as I love Semlak, the city entices me. I want to move to Temeswar or

Arad someday, but as a single mother, I don't know how welcome I will be. So, if you ever to go Amerika, you must take me along.

Your Mammi

Monday, September 19, 1921

My dear child,

Sometimes I hope you're a girl, because then we'll spend a lot of time together cooking. I learned how to cook from my mother, and once each of my three sisters was old enough, they helped, too.

I cooked a lot with my sisters. Eva, who is only two years younger than me, spent many hours in the kitchen with me and Mama. Then we had to teach Anna-Maria and Elisabeth, who were five and six years younger than me, respectively, when Mama was out at the farm. Sometimes it was really hard, because Anna-Maria and Elisabeth wouldn't listen to me and Eva. They wanted to play instead, but we all had to learn the importance of hard work from a young age.

The first thing I would teach you is how to sweep the floor. Once you're old enough to hold a broom, you can sweep. Then you can learn how to wash fruits and vegetables. Once you're eight or nine, you can cook on the stove.

I know you'll prefer to play with your cousins and other kids in the street, just like my sisters did. Mama and Tata will also play with you when

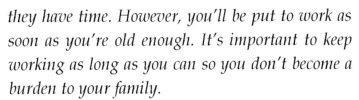

they have time. However, you'll be put to work as soon as you're old enough. It's important to keep working as long as you can so you don't become a burden to your family.

I hope you like my palatschinken. Those are big, flat pancakes. We love to put some plum jam inside, or, on really special occasions, cinnamon and sugar. I can already see your face smothered in plum jam! I just hope you don't eat too many palatschinken – they can cause tummy problems! There was once a girl in our town – I remember hearing this when I was a child – whose Oma had made her too many palatschinken. The poor girl ate them as fast as they landed on her plate, and her Oma cooked them up as fast as her granddaughter could eat them. In the end, the girl got really sick! But don't worry, my dearest child. You have nothing to worry about: your Mammi can't cook that fast!

Your Mammi

September 25, 1921

My dear child,

Today is the anniversary of my grandmother's death. She died of a stroke in 1914. My Omama's name was Elisabeta Wolf, née Stefan. She grew up as an orphan child but had accumulated over three acres of wine gardens and three houses in her life. Omama was widely known as a pious and good woman. She gave birth to 16 children: two were twins, my father and an aunt. I knew one uncle and two aunts: Onkel Martin, Tante Susanna, and Tante Kati, my father's twin. The others had passed away. I never knew my Otata. He died before I was born.

Omama lived with Onkel Martin and Tante Johanna, so we held the funeral in their home. I helped clean out the living room. All the furniture had to be removed to make room for the coffin and the extra chairs and benches from the church. We only left some cupboards in there, because they're too heavy to move.

Many of Tata's former customers came by to express their condolences. Omama's greatest fear had come true: Tata never returned from Amerika before she died. Mama wrote him a letter after the burial. But with Kaiser Ferdinand's death, and Germany declaring war on France earlier that year, I didn't know when my father would make it home.

As you'll get to know, whether someone is born, gets married, or has died in Semlak, the women start baking. The men, of course, pull out the schnapps. Everyone helps prepare for the burial. In death, this also means that people help clean and dress the body. Onkel Martin, Tante Kati, and Tante Susanna chose Omama's best dress for her burial. They made sure to include several underskirts and her best kerchief so she'd look as beautiful as possible.

The next day, so many people came to visit. Of course, Omama's children and all nine grandchildren were there, too.

In the evening, relatives stayed in the living room, with the coffin. Members of the congregation came and sat in one of the other rooms in the house and sang from our hymnal.

I cried a lot. I found great comfort in having so many people there. The hymns repeatedly reminded me that Jesus was with us, too, and that my Omama had now gone to a better place. Even *the cakes that were passed around reminded me of her. As you'll soon learn, no one cooks and bakes better than your Omama.*

The men sat in a separate room and enjoyed their schnapps. I do always wonder what they talk about. When I was younger, I'd ask Tata, but he'd just tell me that I'll find out when I'm older and married. (Of course, as you'll soon know, marriage didn't happen for me.)

The priest visited, too, offered some prayers, and then joined in the singing.

Everyone stayed until about midnight. Onkel Martin and Tante Johanna slept in makeshift beds in another room, and the burial took place the next day.

You will, sadly, lose many people in your life. I'm still young, but I don't believe it gets easier as you get older. I only hope that death doesn't teach you to fear love.

Your Mammi

Saturday, October 1, 1921

My dear child,

Temeswar is a beautiful small city that is about 95 km away from Semlak. I read about it often in our weekly newspaper. They have electric streetlights and trams. There's also a market, of course, and it's much bigger than ours here in Semlak. They even have telephones there. Although…telephones won't be much use to me if they don't have them in Semlak.

I imagine Temeswar to be small enough that I won't feel swallowed up by throngs of people but still big enough that I can see the latest fashions in the stores and enjoy the modern life. I hope to live there someday. (Of course, unless you go to Amerika, as I said before.)

Although the pictures in the newspaper aren't very clear, I can still see that the inside of the Lutheran church is very beautiful. Our faith is important to me, and I hope it will be to you, too. It has helped keep our family together for several centuries. I imagine I'd feel more at home with the Transylvanian Germans in the Carpathians, who are Lutheran, than with the Banater Germans,

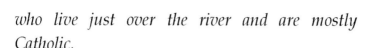

who live just over the river and are mostly
Catholic.

There are Catholic Germans here in Semlak,
too, and we get along with them. They live near
their church, just like most Lutherans live near
ours, and the Calvinists near theirs. We of course
say hello to each other, and we celebrate with each
other when the occasion calls for it. We mourn
with each other, and the churches will ring their
bells together for funerals if a family has members
in more than one church.

But I don't understand why Catholics must go
to their priest to ask God for forgiveness. Should
that not be a personal act, one that remains
between you and God? And why must Catholics
learn Latin to understand their mass? It should be
offered in the local language so that everyone can
understand the Word of God. What do children do
in Catholic churches until they learn Latin?

You will be raised in the Lutheran faith, but
you will also be taught to respect all people.

Your Mammi

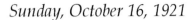

Sunday, October 16, 1921

My dear child,

This morning, a woman crossed the street without looking and was hit really hard by a cyclist. We weren't sure at the start if she'd actually died — she was so still, and with her heavy Sunday clothing on, we couldn't tell right away if she was breathing! It turned out that she was fine, but the incident brought a story to mind that I'd like to share with you.

Once you're born, you'll meet members of the Bartolf family. Our families have known each other for generations. Mama's mother is your Fendt Omi. Her maiden name was Bartolf. She told me this story.

One day, a relative of Omi's, Frau Elisabeth Wagner, née Bartolf, stayed behind at a funeral to help clean up the house while family and friends were at the burial. As she started to remove the sheets from the bed, she realized they were still warm. The person was still alive! So she ran after the funeral procession to tell everyone. Thankfully, they don't nail the coffin closed until after prayers at the gravesite.

I don't know what happened afterwards — the story is already old (Frau Wagner is over 20 years older than I am), and some details have been forgotten. The person may have been really sick and died eventually, anyway. It's not something one asks about, so the end will have to remain a mystery.

I have another request of you: When I die, please make sure my body is cold and that I'm really dead!

Your Mammi

Friday, November 11, 1921

My dear child,

War is a horrible thing. I hope you never experience it. The war already ended three years ago, but we are still feeling its effects.

Our churches still don't have their bells. During the war, when the army needed more metal for cannon, churches across Romania had to donate their bells to be melted down. No matter the religion, the church is the centre of everyone's life. Our town has been quieter since the bells came down.

We lost 51 young men during the war, and life since then has not been good. When I was born, Semlak, our family's home for almost 100 years, was in the Austro-Hungarian Empire. We now belong to Romania. This happened to a lot of the Germans in Hungary. The Transylvanian Saxons in the Carpathian Mountains also belong to Romania now. Some German towns and villages belong to the new country of Yugoslavia. Some are still in Hungary.

Two years ago, in 1919, the church wanted to celebrate the 100th anniversary of our arrival in

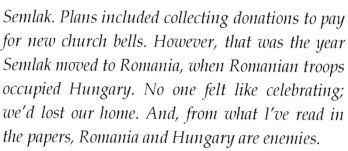

Semlak. Plans included collecting donations to pay for new church bells. However, that was the year Semlak moved to Romania, when Romanian troops occupied Hungary. No one felt like celebrating; we'd lost our home. And, from what I've read in the papers, Romania and Hungary are enemies.

Mama always said that if Empress Sisi were still alive, none of this would have happened. I keep reminding Mama that Empress Sisi would have been very old, and that it was the assassination of Archduke Ferdinand that started the war. But Mama still believes that Empress Sisi could've prevented all of this.

Semlak is only about 15 km from the border. It pains me to know that such a short distance separates us from our true home. The worries are about more than just pride; they are also about practicality. How can I help you with your schooling if your teachers are Romanian? I don't know Romanian. Will your children still be speaking German when they go to school? Or will our German culture slowly disappear?

The change has also affected our economy. Tata said that each country is putting extra charges on grain from outside its borders. We no longer sell our grain to Hungary or Austria, because it costs

them too much to buy it. *This means that the larger farms will start to produce less, so they'll need fewer farmhands, and this will pass down to all the farms here. It will not be easy, but life has never been easy for the Wolf family.*

Your Mammi

Wednesday, November 30, 1921

My dear child,

   As I write this, I can feel fear rise up and my breath quicken. But you also have to understand how precious life is.
   I have already experienced the death of a baby, but not my own. Let me tell you what happened.
   Mama's first child was a boy, born in 1899, and they named him Adam. He's of course still alive. Then I was born, in 1901. Her second son, Martin, was born a year later but with a weak constitution and died the day after his birth. My three sisters were born afterwards. It wasn't until I was ten that Mama had another boy. He was named after Tata: Andreas. Mama and Tata were so happy to have one more child, and I was excited to have a brother I might finally get to tease! I held him every day. When Mama tried to sleep, I would take him out for a walk, and all our friends would comment on how lovely he was and that it was high time that God blessed us with another son.
   But nine days later, he suffered convulsions.
   Watching such a young, helpless baby shake so violently...my child, it's something I hope you'll

never have to witness. I pray to Jesus every day that you will be born safe and healthy and live to see your own children grow up.

Normally, when we have church bells and the small one rings continuously, and then the big bell joins it, you know a child has died in Semlak. The entire town feels sadder that day.

Will God take you from my arms before I'm ready to let go? I hope not. I love you too much already.

Your Mammi

Thursday, December 8, 1921

My dear child,

Today was so frustrating! I had a fight with several in the family. They said I should name you after our parents, as has been our custom for generations. But that makes no sense! I'm already named after my mother — if you are a girl, it makes no sense to have a fourth Katharina in the family, after Mama, Aunt Kati, and me. And naming you Andreas would remind me of the brother I lost and the father who left us for long periods of time for Amerika. The fact that your godfather will be Andreas Fendt does not help me though, since custom dictates that I should name a male child after the godfather if not after my father. My family thinks Andreas is the perfect name for you if you're a boy.

I don't know what name I shall give you if you're a girl. Maybe Elisabeth, after Omama. If you're a boy, though, I think Martin would be nice. I never knew my brother Martin, because I was only one year old when he died. And Uncle Martin looked after Omama. So I have no sad associations with the name, only hopeful ones.

Yes. I think either Elisabeth or Martin would do. What do you think?

Your Mammi

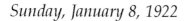

Sunday, January 8, 1922

My dear child,

You're moving around a lot today. It's hard to write! But every time I feel you move, I know I'm one moment closer to seeing your beautiful face. You're coming into the world of a large family who will help look after you.

After you're born, you'll be baptized as soon as possible. If you're sickly when you're born, the midwife will baptize you right away to make sure you're baptized before you die. I pray she doesn't have to do that.

Your godparents and the midwife will take you to Pastor Fröhlich's home to be baptized. I will stay at home so I can recover. I hope you behave for them!

There is one custom I should share with you, if only because it's absurd.

Often, once the godparents have returned with the baby, the godmother will place the baby under the table and call the house cat (even if there is no cat). At that point, the father is supposed to come out and "save" the baby by picking it up from under the table. The father is supposed to demonstrate through this custom that he will be a good father, not a cruel one, because he has saved the baby from being eaten by the cat.

Once your godparents have returned with you, friends and family will help with cooking and they will look after me for a little while so I can heal from your birth.

I'm scared to give birth. There are so many dangers, and so many things can go wrong. But you must come out at some point, right?

I've been crocheting your baptismal bonnet and little jacket. Since you'll be born in the winter, I've made them with thick yarn to make sure you're kept extra warm. Mama is working on your baptismal pillow. It's beautiful. I can only imagine what you'll look like once you're put in it. One of my sisters is working on your baptismal blanket. That should also protect you from the cold wind as you head to the church.

Your Mammi

Friday, January 20, 1922

My dear child,

A mother has two fears: that her child will die young, maybe even before birth, and that she'll die before she's raised her child. As you now know, my Wolf Omama gave birth to 16 children. Only four grew up to become adults, yet somehow she endured and lived to be 76 years old. I think she found her strength in God and Jesus and in serving them.

I don't know if I would have that much strength. I go to church every Sunday, say my prayers, and I do try to be a good person. But the fears I have inside are too real. Can God really make fears like this go away? If He can, why do I have them? Or did Omama simply learn how to live with these fears?

You're my first child, and maybe even my last. You will be well cared for if I die, that much I know. But the thought of not being there for you hurts too much sometimes. I want to make sure you don't grow up an orphan like Omama did. I want you baptized in our Lutheran faith, and I want to see you play with your friends, find a spouse who makes you happy and serves you well, make a good living, and, God willing, have children so that I, too, may be an Omama someday.

I want to make sure you have a healthy and prosperous life. That is my greatest wish for you, my child.

Your Mammi

Katharina's Real Life

In the end, Katharina gave birth to a boy. That's where this story ends, but mine begins almost 80 years later.

In 2001, I was snooping through my grandmother's closets when I chanced upon two boxes of old photos. I asked my grandmother a million questions. She answered as many as she could, but she was already in her 80s; some of those memories existed too far back for her to recall all the details.

In that treasure trove were several postcards by Katharina Wolf, my great grandmother. Most of them were addressed to Mom. Because only one mentions my aunt, who is several years younger, I assume that most were written before she was born. A few postcards also appeared to be earlier correspondence to her son, my grandfather.

We don't know who her son's father was. The church records have a checkmark under a column with the heading *illegitimate*. I have one family portrait where he is a young boy, perhaps three years old. His mother is in the photo, and seated next to her is a man, whose identity has never fully been confirmed. I have pictures of another man who appears to be Katharina's life partner, but I don't know his name either. All I can confirm is that there are no marriage entries for her in the Semlak Lutheran church records. Was she so progressive that she didn't feel she needed to marry? Or did she simply marry in another Lutheran church?

It took some time to read through Katharina's postcards, because although she wrote in German, she often used Hungarian phonetics, especially in the early ones. Here's an example:

One thing became clear, though, as I read these: Katharina wanted her grandchildren to know about her side of their family. So we'll start with Katharina's family.

Katharina's mother, Katharina Wolf, née Fendt, was born on April 1, 1878. (For ease of reference, I'll refer to this Katharina by her maiden name.) There is no record of her death in the Semlak Lutheran church books. Katharina mentions a great grandmother in one of her postcards to Mom, though, leading me to believe Katharina Fendt lived into her 80s. Katharina wrote that her mother also cried when she saw pictures of her great grandchildren.

Between the ages of 21 and 33, Katharina Fendt had seven children. Five appear to have lived into adulthood, though dates of death for all of her daughters, Eva, Anna-Maria, Elisabeth, and of course Katharina, are unknown. Her son, Adam, died in 1953.

Katharina's father, Andreas Wolf, was born on January 26, 1876, and died on April 5, 1934, in Semlak. The entry in the church books says he suffered from cardiac issues. Katharina wrote that he travelled to the United States. She doesn't say exactly when but says that Andreas' mother, Elisabeth Wolf, née Stefan, never saw him again before she died, which was in 1914. Ship manifests from Ellis Island show a record for an Andras (no e) Wolf, born in Semlak, who

arrived in New York City on August 1, 1913. This fits except for one detail: the record says this Andras Wolf was born in 1873. There were no other Andreas Wolfs in the Lutheran or Calvinist church records whose age neared Andreas Wolf's. The ship's manifest further details that he had been in the United States before, namely in 1907/1908. Katharina Fendt and Andreas Wolf had no children between 1907 and 1911. For the 1913 trip, the final destination was Harrisburg, Pennsylvania, to visit a Georg Schütt. Andreas's grandmother was a Schütt. All of this suggests it was this Andreas, except for the birth year.

Andreas had a twin, also named Katharina. She was apparently referred to as Kati. In one of her postcards to Mom, Katharina wrote that Kati worked until age 79. Retirement didn't appear to be an option for these people, and I believe the thought of relaxing and enjoying life after a certain age may have even been frowned upon. I have several pictures of Kati, but otherwise I know very little about her.

According to the church books, Andreas and Kati were born in 1876. Andreas died in 1934 at the age of 58. Kati died in 1954 at the age of 78. The original church records attest to these dates.

I've already mentioned the curious entry in an Ellis Island record that says that an Andras Wolf from Semlak was born in 1873. To add to this mystery, Katharina wrote in a postcard that Kati died when she was 81. If you subtract 81 from 1954, you get 1873.

In the end, there will likely never be an answer to this age discrepancy. But it does exist.

So far as I know, all of the descendants of Katharina and her siblings had moved out of Romania by the 1980s. Very few Germans live in Semlak anymore nowadays.

Katharina thought very highly of her grandmother, Elisabeta Wolf, so much so that she dedicated one densely written postcard to her (the writing sample on page 30). According to Katharina, Elisabeth grew up as an orphan child. The Semlak Lutheran church records have no entry for her parents or her birth, so I can't confirm this. The church records say, though, that she died from a stroke on September 25, 1914, at the age of 78. This photo was taken in either 1913 (written on the back in pencil under all the pen) or 1914 (written on the front). Standing next to Elisabeta is Kati.

Looking at Elisabeta's family details in the church records does bring about a point of sadness. In this day and age, I cannot fathom giving birth to 14 children, to see only four grow up. However, child mortality back then was very high. (Katharina wrote 16, but the church records listed 14.)

My ancestors of this time also had a naming custom that we would find odd nowadays, maybe even distasteful or gruesome. Children were commonly named after a member of the family, often starting with the parents, then the godparents, and onwards. If a child died in its early years, often the next child of the same sex was given that name. So it came to pass that Elisabeta Wolf had four daughters named Elisabeth, each one named after her when the

first daughter bearing her name died. Sadly, not even the last one survived.

Everyone I've mentioned in this book did indeed live. If a person was not named, then that person's role in the story was fabricated.

For example, the story about the not-yet-dead person in the coffin did happen. However, the beginning of that journal entry, where a woman was hit by a cyclist, was fictional.

This is Elizabeth Wagner, née Bartolf. Her granddaughter, Rose Mary Keller-Hughes, graciously permitted me to include the story of

the living person about to be buried. Elizabeth Wagner lived from 1877-1950.

There were several marriages between the Bartolf and Wolf families over the years, so I'm confident the families knew each other.

The story about the child who got sick from the palatschinken was something that had happened to me when I was 12 or so. My grandmothers and great grandmothers often made these delicious, heavy crepes for my sister and me. On one fateful afternoon or evening, though, my paternal grandmother and I simply got faster and faster at cooking and eating them, respectively. I didn't want to make her wait for me, and she didn't want to make me wait for her. In the end, I had eaten 10 or 12 of these heavy, oily crepes, which I'd liberally sprinkled with cinnamon and sugar. By that night, I had terrible pains that landed me on the x-ray table in a hospital: my father had feared an appendicitis attack.

It turned out to be a gas pocket. I had eaten too fast.

Of course, exactly what people did and said will never be known. The information about customs, such as burials and baptisms, was taken from the Semlaker Heimatbriefe (Semlak

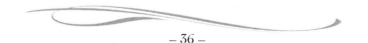

Newsletters) of the Heimatortsgemeinschaft Semlak, a small organization with charitable status in Germany dedicated to preserving the history of this village and its German inhabitants. Other details were taken from Keller-Hughes's book about her family's history.

There are many mysteries about Katharina's life to which we will never find the answer. According to Mom, all the paperwork had been completed to have Katharina reunite with her family in Canada. Unfortunately, she died before she left. But I think she'd be very happy to know that her son lived into his 60s and had two daughters who in turn had two children each. Two of the children already have two children each, too.

Opa Wolf died when I was eight. I felt very close to him, and his death deeply affected me for another 20 years or so. He was the only connection I would have had to his side of the family. Thanks to my great grandmother's courage at writing when she knew she couldn't write well, all of her grandchildren, great grandchildren, and great great grandchildren can now read her story.

And it all started with some postcards in a closet.

Photos

The following picture was taken in 1934 and was Katharina's most special one. She wrote, "Dear children [her son and daughter-in-law], take care of this picture until the young one is 18, so that she can understand it. This is my most treasured one. I send it with tears."

The deceased is Andreas Wolf, her father.

1) Katharina Wolf, née Fendt, Katharina's mother

2) Eva, one of Katharina's sisters

3) Katharina, age 33

4) Adam, Katharina's brother

5) Elisabeth, another sister

6) Kati, Andreas' twin sister

7) Adam, Adam's older son

8) Josef, Adam's younger son

9) Elisabeth's son, Niki

10) Katharina Wolf, née Asztalos, Adam's wife

11) Leni Vogel, sister-in-law to Katharina's mom

12) Lutz. I don't know who he is, but Katharina writes that he ran away from the family.

Katharina is sixteen years old in this photo. Young, unmarried women did not cover their hair in her culture. She's wearing a traditional outfit.

Katharina describes herself on the back of this photo as "a young woman." She's wearing a modern dress.

Katharina wrote on the back of this photo that she's wearing a traditional Romanian costume. Therefore, this photo was likely taken after 1919.

Here's a family photo. The woman with the kerchief is Katharina's mom. Katharina is standing in the middle, and the handsome man to her right is her grown-up son, Martin. I don't know the names of the young boy or the man seated on the far right, but they may be a nephew and brother-in-law, respectively.

Katharina had written a birthday greeting on the back of this photo to Mom. The man next to her is her partner, but we don't know his name or if they ever married.

Katharina describes the girl in this photo as a "young bride" who had just participated in the Catholic sacrament of confirmation. The photo is in front of the cathedral in Temeswar. Katharina mentions my aunt on the back of this photo, so it was likely taken in the late 50s or very early 60s.

Bibliography

Berglund, Sten, and Frank Aarebrot. *The Political History of Eastern Europe in the 20th Century.* Lyme: Edward Elgar Publishing, Inc., 1997.

Heimatortsgemeinschaft Semlak. *Heimatbrief Archiv ab Nr. 20.* http://www.semlak.de/heimatbrief/archiv-ab-nr-20.html (accessed Oct 2015).

Held, Joseph. *The Columbia History of Eastern Europe in the Twentieth Century.* Edited by Joseph Held. New York: Columbia University Press, 1992.

Keller-Hughes, Rose Mary. *Roots and Branches.* Unknown: Self-published, 2006.

McKim Pharr, Jody. *History.* 02 09, 2012. http://www.dvhh.org/temesquarters/history.htm (accessed 09 2015).

Schmidt, Georg. Familienbuch der Evangelischen Kirchengemeinde Semlak. Heimatortsgemeinschaft Semlak, 2003.

Sur, Iulia. *Einzige evangelisch-lutherische Kirche in Temeswar.* 08 26, 2015. http://www.adz.ro/artikel/artikel/einzige-evangelisch-lutherische-kirche-in-temeswar/ (accessed 09 2015).

Tullius, Nick. *Banat Timeline.* 02 10, 2015. http://www.dvhh.org/alexanderhausen/history/banat-timeline.htm (accessed 10 2015).